DINO EXPLORERS

FIERCE DINOSAURS

Pachycephalosaurs and Ceratopsians

Clare Hibbert

Enslow Publishing
101 W. 23rd Street
Suite 240
New York, NY 10011
USA
enslow.com

Published in 2019 by Enslow Publishing, LLC
101 W. 23rd Street, Suite 240, New York, NY 10011

Cataloging-in-Publication Data

Names: Hibbert, Clare.
Title: Fierce Dinosaurs: Pachycephalosaurs and Ceratopsians / Clare Hibbert.
Description: New York : Enslow Publishing, 2019. | Series: Dino explorers | Includes glossary
and index.
Identifiers: ISBN 9781978500099 (pbk.) | ISBN 9781978500082 (library bound) | ISBN
9781978500105 (6 pack.) | ISBN 9781978500112 (ebook)
Subjects: LCSH: Pachycephalosaurus--Juvenile literature. | Ceratopsidae--Juvenile literature. |
Dinosaurs--Juvenile literature.
Classification: LCC QE862.O65 H53 2019 | DDC 567.914--dc23

Printed in the United States of America

To Our Readers: We have done our best to make sure all website addresses
in this book were active and appropriate when we went to press. However,
the author and the publisher have no control over and assume no
liability for the material available on those websites or on any websites
they may link to. Any comments or suggestions can be sent by email to
customerservice@enslow.com.

Excerpts and articles have been reproduced with the permission of the
copyright holders.

CONTENTS

The Dinosaur Age

Dinosaurs appeared around 225 million years ago (mya) and ruled the land for over 160 million years. At the same time (the Mesozoic Era), marine reptiles and pterosaurs ruled the oceans and skies.

This family tree shows when various dinosaurs appeared and and how they were related. As new fossils are found, paleontologists often change their minds about the groupings.

Dinosaurs suddenly died out 65 mya, along with marine reptiles, pterosaurs and many other animals. A huge meteorite probably hit Earth, throwing up dust that blocked out the Sun for months.

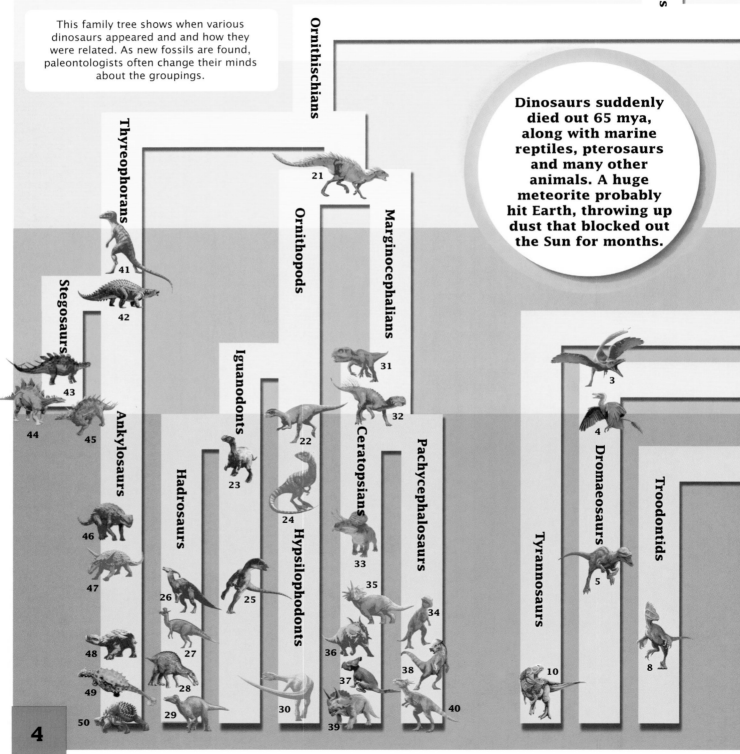

KEY

1. *Herrerasaurus*	11. *Melanorosaurus*	21. *Heterodontosaurus*	31. *Yinlong*	41. *Scutellosaurus*
2. *Allosaurus*	12. *Plateosaurus*	22. *Hypsilophodon*	32. *Psittacosaurus*	42. *Scelidosaurus*
3. *Archaeopteryx*	13. *Mamenchisaurus*	23. *Iguanodon*	33. *Zuniceratops*	43. *Tuojiangosaurus*
4. *Microraptor*	14. *Brachiosaurus*	24. *Leaellynasaura*	34. *Stegoceras*	44. *Stegosaurus*
5. *Deinonychus*	15. *Amargasaurus*	25. *Gasparinisaura*	35. *Styracosaurus*	45. *Kentrosaurus*
6. *Spinosaurus*	16. *Nigersaurus*	26. *Parasaurolophus*	36. *Achelousaurus*	46. *Minmi*
7. *Giganotosaurus*	17. *Sauroposeidon*	27. *Lambeosaurus*	37. *Protoceratops*	47. *Sauropelta*
8. *Troodon*	18. *Argentinosaurus*	28. *Shantungosaurus*	38. *Pachycephalosaurus*	48. *Edmontonia*
9. *Therizinosaurus*	19. *Saltasaurus*	29. *Edmontosaurus*	39. *Triceratops*	49. *Euoplocephalus*
10. *Tyrannosaurus*	20. *Rapetosaurus*	30. *Thescelosaurus*	40. *Stygimoloch*	50. *Ankylosaurus*

Saurischians

Theropods

Allosaurs

Sauropods

Prosauropods

Diplodocids

Spinosaurs

Titanosaurs

Therizinosaurs

Triassic
251–206 mya

Jurassic
206–145 mya

Cretaceous
145–65 mya

5

Yinlong

The best-known of the ceratopsians (dinosaurs with horned faces) is *Triceratops* (pages 22–23), who lived during the Late Cretaceous. However, the first dinosaurs in this group appeared much earlier. *Yinlong* is the oldest, most primitive ceratopsian that is known.

Ceratopsian Characteristics

Plant-eating *Yinlong* did not have the dramatic horns of later ceratopsians, or much of a frill. It is counted as part of the family because of its parrot-like beak, formed by a bony lump on its upper jaw. Later ceratopsians were much larger and moved on all fours, but *Yinlong* was small, bipedal, and speedy.

Yinlong had three-fingered hands at the end of short, slim arms. It had chunky, muscular back legs.

Yinlong had a deep, wide skull. The tip of the snout was like a parrot's beak.

Made in China

Chinese paleontologist Xu Xing has named more dinosaurs than any living paleontologist. *Yinlong* and *Guanlong* owe their names to him, as well as the therizinosaur *Beipiaosaurus*, dromaeosaur *Sinornithosaurus,* and birdlike *Mei.*

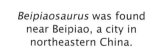

Beipiaosaurus was found near Beipiao, a city in northeastern China.

PERIOD	TRIASSIC	JURASSIC	CRETACEOUS	AGE OF MAMMALS
MILLIONS OF YEARS AGO	251	206 · 158 · 145	65	present

Name: *Yinlong* (YIN-long)
Family: Ceratopsidae
Height: 1.5 feet (0.5 m)
Length: 3.9 feet (1.2 m)
Weight: 33 pounds (15 kg)

DINOSAUR PROFILE

The tyrannosaur *Guanlong* preyed on *Yinlong*. It was alive earlier than its American cousin *Tyrannosaurus*. It was smaller, too—just 3.3 feet (1 meter) tall.

Sinornithosaurus was only the fifth feathered dinosaur to be discovered.

Psittacosaurus

Another early ceratopsian, *Psittacosaurus* lived in eastern Asia in the Early Cretaceous. Its name means "parrot lizard." Paleontologists have uncovered and studied hundreds of *Psittacosaurus* fossils and identified at least 14 different species.

Differences and Similarities

Psittacosaurus varied in size—the smallest species was a third smaller than the largest—but they were all roughly the same shape. They had a distinctive, rounded skull that could have housed a large brain. They also had large eye sockets. Paleontologists think that *Psittacosaurus* had good senses of sight and smell.

Psittacosaurus had defensive horns sticking out from its cheeks.

It is possible that only some species had tail bristles, or even just some individuals.

Bristled Tail

In 2002 paleontologists announced the discovery of the most perfectly preserved *Psittacosaurus* fossil yet. It had very detailed skin impressions and, excitingly, 6.3-inch (16-cm) bristles on its tail. Since then, more individuals with bristles have been found.

This fossil shows the bristles sticking out from the tail.

PERIOD	TRIASSIC	JURASSIC	CRETACEOUS	AGE OF MAMMALS
MILLIONS OF YEARS AGO	251	206	145	65	present

112

Name: *Psittacosaurus*
(SIT-uh-ko-SAWR-us)
Family: Psittacosauridae
Height: 2 feet (0.6 m)
Length: 6.6 feet (2 m)
Weight: 44 pounds (20 kg)

DINOSAUR PROFILE

Psittacosaurus's rounded and flattened beak was strong enough to crack tough seeds and nuts.

Birdlike *Sinovenator* hunted in packs. It was a troodontid.

Zuniceratops

Sometimes called the missing link between the early ceratopsians and the later ones, *Zuniceratops* had a large frill, and two brow horns, but no nose horn. It lived in what is now New Mexico about ten million years before its nose-horned cousins appeared.

Face Features

Zuniceratops had a long snout with a bony ridge along it. It fed on cones, shrubs, and bark, which it stripped from tree trunks with its beaky mouth. Its cheek bones stuck out to the sides, and might have been tipped with tiny horns.

The Fringed Heads

Zuniceratops and the ceratopsians belonged to a group of dinosaurs called the marginocephalians, or "fringed heads," that had a thick, bony fringe at the back of the skull. The pachycephalosaurs were marginocephalians, too. Named after *Pachycephalosaurus* (pages 20–21), they include *Stegoceras* (pages 12–13) and *Stygimoloch* (pages 24–25).

Zuniceratops is the earliest known ceratopsian with brow horns.

PERIOD	TRIASSIC	JURASSIC	CRETACEOUS	AGE OF MAMMALS

91

MILLIONS OF YEARS AGO

251   206   145   65   present

Name: *Zuniceratops*
(ZOO-nee-SEH-ruh-tops)
Family: Ceratopsidae
Height: 3.3 feet (1 m)
Length: 11.5 feet (3.5 m)
Weight: 330 pounds (150 kg)

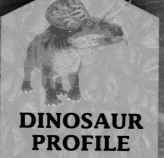

DINOSAUR PROFILE

Zuniceratops is named after the Zuni people, a tribe of Native Americans that live in New Mexico.

Zuniceratops is known from just one skull and a handful of other bones.

The brow horns carried on growing throughout its life.

Holes in the frill bone kept it as light as possible. A solid frill would have made the skull too heavy for the neck to support.

***Zuniceratops* walked on all fours. It probably lived in herds to protect itself against theropods.**

Stegoceras

A small, bipedal plant eater, *Stegoceras* lived in North America around 75 mya. As in all pachycephalosaurs (thick-headed dinosaurs), *Stegoceras*'s skull had extra-thick bone at the top. Its name means "horn roof."

With big eyes and complex nasal cavaties, *Stegoceras* would have had good senses of sight and smell.

Dome Details

Stegoceras's skull dome would have protected the brain if the dinosaur charged headfirst. Most experts no longer believe that pachycephalosaurs fought each other head-to-head, but they could have still headbutted attackers and rivals. Perhaps the dome also helped to identify *Stegoceras* males and females or may have been used for display.

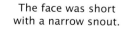

The face was short with a narrow snout.

PERIOD	TRIASSIC	JURASSIC	CRETACEOUS	AGE OF MAMMALS

75

MILLIONS OF YEARS AGO

251 · 206 · 145 · 65 · present

Name: *Stegoceras*
  (Steg-OSS-er-us)
Family: Ceratopsidae
Height: 2.1 feet (0.6 m)
Length: 7.4 feet (2.3 m)
Weight: 66 pounds (30 kg)

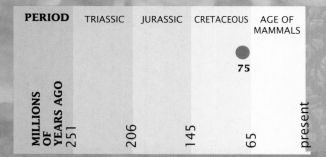

The skull probably started out flat and became more domed as *Stegoceras* grew.

First Fossils

Stegoceras fossils were first discovered in the Dinosaur Park Formation by the Canadian paleontologist Lawrence Lambe. It is one of the earliest-known pachycephalosaurs. Teeth found near the first find were also thought to belong to *Stegoceras*, but were later identified as belonging to a very different dinosaur— *Troodon*.

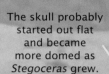

Stegoceras's back legs were about three times longer than its arms.

Early reconstructions show *Stegoceras* with a straight neck. In reality, it was curved.

Styracosaurus

Unlike its cousin *Triceratops* (pages 22–23), *Styracosaurus* did not battle by locking horns. It did not even have brow horns. However, it did have an impressive nose horn and a showy selection of spikes around its neck frill.

Weighty Attacker

Styracosaurus's name means "spiked lizard." The size and condition of its spikes were important for impressing possible mates and scaring off rivals. Faced with an enemy, *Styracosaurus* probably charged at it side-on, relying on its powerful shoulders and all the force of its 3.3-ton (3-t) body.

Styracosaurus may have pumped blood into its fleshy frill to "blush." This could have been a signal to others of its species that it was ready to mate.

Shared Environment

Herbivorous *Styracosaurus* was another dinosaur discovered in Canada's Dinosaur Park Formation. Other ceratopsians also lived in its habitat of swamps and floodplains, including *Centrosaurus* and *Chasmosaurus*. Predators included the tyrannosaurs *Albertosaurus* and *Gorgosaurus*.

Fearsome tyrannosaur *Albertosaurus* preyed on young *Styracosaurus*.

PERIOD	TRIASSIC	JURASSIC	CRETACEOUS	AGE OF MAMMALS
MILLIONS OF YEARS AGO	251	206	145	65	present

75

Name: *Styracosaurus*
(Stih-RAK-uh-SAWR-us)
Family: Ceratopsidae
Height: 6 feet (1.8 m)
Length: 18 feet (5.5 m)
Weight: 3.3 tons (3 t)

DINOSAUR PROFILE

Hollow "windows" in the bone kept the neck frill light.

Styracosaurus had a tall, straight nose horn but no brow horns.

The neck frill had at least four pairs of long spikes. There could be smaller spikes at the base of the frill, too.

Styracosaurus's short, stubby legs supported a bulky body, like a rhino's.

Achelousaurus

Achelousaurus was a medium-sized ceratopsian that lived in North America in the Late Cretaceous. It had two short cheek spikes and a pair of longer spikes at the top of its neck frill.

Wavy-Edged Frill

Achelousaurus belonged to the group of ceratopsians known as the centrosaurines, which were named after *Centrosaurus*. Their name, meaning "pointed lizards," refers to their distinguishing feature—the small hornlets dotted around the edge of their neck frill.

Achelousaurus had raised bony areas, called bosses, along its snout and above its eyes.

PERIOD	TRIASSIC	JURASSIC	CRETACEOUS	AGE OF MAMMALS

74.5

MILLIONS OF YEARS AGO
251 · 206 · 145 · 65 · present

Name: *Achelousaurus*
(Ah-KEL-oo-SAWR-us)
Family: Ceratopsidae
Height: 8.9 feet (2.7 m)
Length: 20 feet (6 m)
Weight: 3.3 tons (3 t)

DINOSAUR PROFILE

Achelousaurus's skull was more than 5.2 feet (1.6 m) long from the tip of its spikes to the end of its beaky snout.

Horns and Lumps

Achelousaurus was closely related to another ceratopsian, *Einiosaurus*. Both had spiky frill margins and two longer spikes at the top of the frill; both had bony lumps, or bosses, instead of brow horns. *Einiosaurus* still had a nose horn—it curved downward very distinctively. *Achelousaurus* had a bony lump on its nose instead of a horn.

This *Achelousaurus* skull was dug up in Montana in 1985 by the American paleontologist Jack Horner.

Achelousaurus used its ridged, parrot-like beak to break off tough plant stems.

Protoceratops

A spectacular fossil discovered in 1971 in the Gobi Desert, Mongolia, captured two dinosaurs locked in combat. They had been buried alive. One was the plant-eating, primitive ceratopsian *Protoceratops*; the other was the dromaeosaur *Velociraptor*.

Protoceratops and *Velociraptor* had been preserved in sand mid-fight. Experts believe they were caught up in a sudden sandstorm.

Life in the Gobi

Many *Protoceratops* specimens have been found in the red sandstone of the Gobi Desert, including fossilized nests, eggs, and babies. During the Late Cretaceous, the Gobi was not as dry as it is now. There were probably seasonal floods.

Protoceratops used its wide, spade-like claws to dig nests and burrows. It laid up to 15 eggs at a time.

Like all dromaeosaurs, *Velociraptor* had a killer curved claw on the second toe of each foot. It slashed at prey to make it bleed to death.

PERIOD	TRIASSIC	JURASSIC	CRETACEOUS	AGE OF MAMMALS
MILLIONS OF YEARS AGO	251	206	145	65 — present

73

Name: *Protoceratops*
(Pro-toe-SEH-ruh-tops)
Family: Ceratopsidae
Height: 2.3 feet (0.7 m)
Length: 6.2 feet (1.9 m)
Weight: 397 pounds (180 kg)

DINOSAUR PROFILE

This fossil of a newly hatched *Protoceratops andrewsi* was discovered in 1997.

Desert Discoveries

The first *Protoceratops* specimens were discovered in the 1920s by American paleontologist Roy Chapman Andrews, so they were given the species name *andrewsi*. In 2001, a second species was identified, *Protoceratops hellenikorhinus*. Unlike *Protoceratops andrewsi*, it had two nose horns, but no front teeth.

Protoceratops had a relatively large neck frill, probably for display.

Velociraptor was about the same size as *Protoceratops*.

Protoceratops's tough, horny beak was not powerful enough to damage Velociraptor.

Pachycephalosaurus

The pachycephalosaurs are named after *Pachycephalosaurus*, a dome-headed dinosaur from Late Cretaceous North America. Paleontologists once thought that these plant-eaters bashed their heads together like goats. However, it is unlikely that they fought each other head-to-head.

Pachycephalosaurus walked and ran on two legs, but would have foraged on all fours.

Protective Helmet

The solid bone at the top of the skull protected *Pachycephalosaurus*'s delicate brain when it charged headfirst at full speed. The bone was 10 inches (25 cm) thick in places.

Pachycephalosaurus's jaw had tiny, sharp teeth for eating soft fruit, seeds, and young leaves.

PERIOD	TRIASSIC	JURASSIC	CRETACEOUS	AGE OF MAMMALS
MILLIONS OF YEARS AGO	251	206	145 · 68	65 · present

Name: *Pachycephalosaurus* (Pak-ee-SEF-uh-lo-SAWR-us)
Family: Pachycephalosauridae
Height: 5.9 feet (1.8 m)
Length: 15 feet (4.5 m)
Weight: 992 pounds (450 kg)

DINOSAUR PROFILE

Pachycephalosaurus used its head to charge into rivals' thighs.

Large eyes gave *Pachycephalosaurus* good binocular vision.

There was a circle of bony spikes around the bottom of the skull dome; there were also spikes at the end of the snout.

Pachycephalosaurus had long legs and short arms. It was not a fast runner.

Fossil Discoveries

Pachycephalosaurus was named in 1931. Not many fossils have been found—just one skull, some skull roofs, and a few other bones. In 2016, paleontologists announced that they had found skulls from two baby *Pachycephalosaurus* at the Hell Creek Formation in Montana.

Triceratops

One of the biggest ceratopsians, *Triceratops* lived right at the end of the Cretaceous in what is now North America. Its most striking feature was its three horns—a longer pair above its eyes and a shorter one on its nose.

Skull Features

Triceratops's skull was massive. Its horns and neck frill were both used for display—showing off to possible mates, fighting rivals, and perhaps even allowing herd members to identify each other. The dinosaur also used its horns to defend against predatory tyrannosaurs.

Triceratops's skull was around 6.6 feet (2 m) long—about a quarter of its total body length.

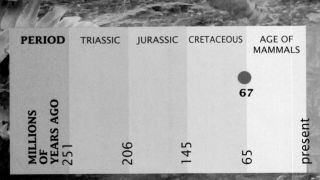

PERIOD	TRIASSIC	JURASSIC	CRETACEOUS	AGE OF MAMMALS
MILLIONS OF YEARS AGO	251	206	145	65	present

67

Name: *Triceratops*
(Try-SEH-ruh-tops)
Family: Ceratopsidae
Height: 10 feet (3 m)
Length: 28 feet (8.5 m)
Weight: 8.8 tons (8 t)

DINOSAUR PROFILE

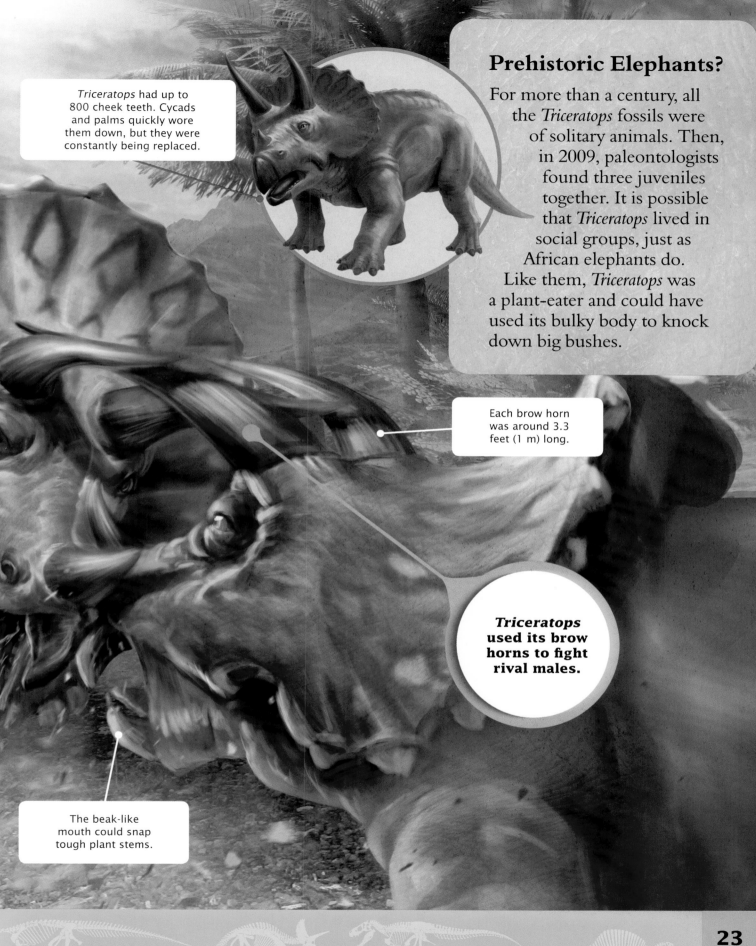

Triceratops had up to 800 cheek teeth. Cycads and palms quickly wore them down, but they were constantly being replaced.

Prehistoric Elephants?

For more than a century, all the *Triceratops* fossils were of solitary animals. Then, in 2009, paleontologists found three juveniles together. It is possible that *Triceratops* lived in social groups, just as African elephants do. Like them, *Triceratops* was a plant-eater and could have used its bulky body to knock down big bushes.

Each brow horn was around 3.3 feet (1 m) long.

Triceratops used its brow horns to fight rival males.

The beak-like mouth could snap tough plant stems.

Stygimoloch

Discovered in the Hell Creek Formation of Montana, *Stygimoloch* was first described in 1983. Since then, paleontologists have argued about whether this plant-eating pachycephalosaur is a species in its own right or just a juvenile version of *Pachycephalosaurus* (pages 20–21).

Bizarre Beast

Like *Pachycephalosaurus*, *Stygimoloch* had a dome-shaped skull surrounded by bony horns. It had more horny bumps on the top of its snout. Its otherworldly appearance is reflected in its name, which combines "Styx," the river of the dead in Greek mythology, and "Moloch," a Canaanite god worshipped in the Middle East around 1500–1000 BCE.

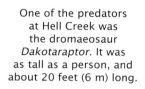

One of the predators at Hell Creek was the dromaeosaur *Dakotaraptor*. It was as tall as a person, and about 20 feet (6 m) long.

Stygimoloch's skull was about 18 inches (46 cm) long.

This part of *Stygimoloch*'s skull, shows off some of its horns.

Horns and Growth

American dinosaur expert Jack Horner was one of the first to suggest that *Stygimoloch* was a young *Pachycephalosaurus*. He also thought that *Dracorex* was an earlier growth stage of the same dinosaur. *Pachycephalosaurus* had fewer horns than *Dracorex* or *Stygimoloch*. If Horner's argument is true, it must mean that the dinosaur lost horns as it aged, but that its dome grew larger.

PERIOD	TRIASSIC	JURASSIC	CRETACEOUS	AGE OF MAMMALS
MILLIONS OF YEARS AGO	251	206	145	65	present

66

Name: *Stygimoloch*
(Stij-ih-MOL-ock)
Family: Pachycephalosauridae
Height: 4 feet (1.2 m)
Length: 10 feet (3 m)
Weight: 172 pounds (78 kg)

DINOSAUR PROFILE

Stygimoloch had a cluster of spikes at the back of the head. There was one pair of longer spikes, up to 5.9 inches (15 cm) long, and a few smaller ones.

Stygimoloch had spikes on its cheeks, too, perhaps for protection.

Fun Facts

Now that you have discovered some amazing fierce dinosaurs, boost your knowledge with these 10 quick facts about them!

Yinlong was discovered in the Chinese province where a movie called *Crouching Tiger, Hidden Dragon* (2000) was filmed. Its name means "hidden dragon."

Early Cretaceous rocks in East Asia contain so many *Psittacosaurus* fossils that they are called the *Psittacosaurus biochron*.

The first *Zuniceratops* fossil was found by an eight-year-old boy!

Two species of *Stegoceras* have been discovered—one lived in the far north, in Alberta, Canada, and one was found in New Mexico.

No one is sure how tall *Styracosaurus'* nose horn was. It may have been up to 2 feet (60 cm) long.

Achelousaurus was named after the Greek river god Achelous, whose bull-like horns were pulled off by the hero Heracles.

The theropod *Oviraptor* got its name, meaning "egg thief," because experts once thought—mistakenly—that it stole *Protoceratops* eggs.

Pachycephalosaurus is the largest-known pachycephalosaur.

Some fossils of Triceratops skulls have *Tyrannosaurus* bite marks!

There is one species of *Dracorex*—*Dracorex hogwartsia* ("dragon king of Hogwarts"). It is named after the school of magic in the Harry Potter books.

Your Questions Answered

We know an incredible amount of facts about dinosaurs, even though they lived millions of years ago. Scientists are always finding out new details and unearthing fossils that teach us about the history of life on Earth. Every new discovery answers some questions and leads scientists to ask new ones. Here are some fascinating questions about dinosaurs that scientists now know the answers to.

Coprolites (fossilized dinosaur dung) have helped us understand more about dinosaurs' diets.

How much do we know about dinosaurs' diets?

Scientists are still discovering many details about different dinosaurs' diets. Mostly, they study fossilized teeth and jaws to work out whether the dinosaur ate plants or meat. However, there are other, more exact ways of discovering what each dinosaur species dined on. Coprolites are fossilized dung that reveal in some detail what various dinosaurs digested. Thanks to coprolites, we know that some ate rotten wood, while others, who were plant eaters, had a snack of shellfish every now and then.

Do we know what the skin of dinosaurs looked like?

Until recently, we didn't know exactly what dinosaurs looked like, or even whether they had smooth skin, scales, or feathers. But thanks to a newly developed technique for analyzing fossilized skin pigments, we now have a lot more insight. Skin pigments are the microscopic particles that are responsible for the hues and markings on an animal's skin. In one fossil find of *Psittacosaurus* (see pages 8–9), these pigments were so well preserved that scientists were able to produce a model of the dinosaur that is the most precise to date.

How do scientists know where to look for dinosaur fossils?

Once a scientist has decided what kind of fossil they would like to find, they need to work out what age the rock is that the fossil might be in. Detailed geological maps, showing the age of rock layers, help the scientist work out where they need to start their search. Usually, scientists will try to find areas where the rock they need is on or close to the surface.

Geological maps show the layers of different rock and when they formed.

What do we know about how dinosaurs fought each other?

Apart from predatory attacks (see pages 18–19), dinosaurs also fought each other over territory, mates, and food sources. Dinosaur fossils can tell us a lot about which dinosaurs fought others, even of their own species, and what that involved. For example, some fossils show where bones have healed from what can only have been battle wounds. Other fossils have been found where an attacker's tooth was still lodged in the dinosaur's skull!

Ostriches produce sounds in their throats while keeping their beaks shut.

Do we know what dinosaurs sounded like?

We can't know for sure what dinosaurs sounded like, because the organs used for producing sound were too soft to fossilize. However, scientists have closely studied dinosaurs' living ancestors—birds and crocodiles—and believe that many dinosaurs probably produced sounds in a similar way to today's large birds. Rather than roar, dinosaurs such as *Tyrannosaurus rex* might have made "closed-mouth sounds" like ostriches and cassowaries do.

Glossary

binocular vision Sight that uses two eyes with overlapping fields of view. This allows for good depth perception.

biochron A layer of rock named after the fossil animal or plant that most commonly occurs in it.

bipedal Walking upright on the back legs.

canaanite Relating to an area of ancient Palestine.

ceratopsian A marginocephalian with (usually) horns and frills. Early species were bipedal; later ones were large and quadrupedal.

Cretaceous period The time from 145 to 65 mya, and the third of the periods that make up the Mesozoic Era.

Dinosaur Park Formation A layer of rock in Alberta, Canada, where many well-preserved fossils have been found.

fossil The remains of an animal or plant that died long ago, preserved in rock.

frill A bony area around a dinosaur's neck.

herbivore A plant-eater.

Jurassic period The time from 206 to 145 mya, and the second of the periods that make up the Mesozoic Era.

juvenile A young person or animal.

Mesozoic Era The period of geological time from 251 to 65 million years ago.

mya Short for "millions of years ago."

pachycephalosaur A bipedal marginocephalian with a thick skull.

paleontologist A scientist who studies fossils.

predator An animal that hunts and eats other animals for food.

prey An animal that is hunted and eaten by other animals for food.

species One particular type of living thing. Members of the same species look similar and can produce offspring together.

theropod A bipedal saurischian dinosaur with sharp teeth and claws.

Triassic period The time from 251 to 206 mya, and the first of the periods that make up the Mesozoic Era.

troodontid A birdlike theropod with long legs and good senses.

tyrannosaur A large theropod with a huge head and relatively small arms.

Further Information

BOOKS

Dixon, Dougal. *The Complete Illustrated Encyclopedia of Dinosaurs and Prehistoric Creatures.* London, UK: Hermes House, 2015.

Holtz, Thomas R. *Digging for Triceratops: A Discovery Timeline.* North Mankato, MN: Capstone Press, 2015.

Jackson, Tom. *The Magnificent Book of Dinosaurs and Other Prehistoric Creatures.* San Diego, CA: Silver Dolphin, 2016

Naish, Darren and Paul Barrett. *Dinosaurs: How They Lived and Evolved.* Washington, DC: Smithsonian Books, 2016.

WEBSITES

discoverykids.com/category/dinosaurs/
This Discovery Kids site has tons of awesome information about dinosaurs, plus lots of fun games and exciting videos!

kids.nationalgeographic.com/explore/nature/dinosaurs/
Check out this National Geographic site to learn more about dinosaurs.

www.amnh.org/explore/ology/paleontology
This website by the American Museum for Natural History is filled with dinosaur quizzes, information, and activities!

Index